BAD GIRLS

SIRENS, JEZEBELS,

MURDERESSES, THIEVES

& OTHER FEMALE VILLAINS

BAD GIRLS

SIRENS, JEZEBELS,
MURDERESSES, THIEVES
& OTHER FEMALE VILLAINS

JANE YOLEN
HEIDI E. Y. STEMPLE

ILLUSTRATED BY
REBECCA GUAY

ini Charlesbridge

TO THE STEMPLE BAD GIRLS, YOUNG AND OLD,

ESPECIALLY MADDI AND GLENNY.

AND FOR JUDY O'MALLEY—THE BADDEST . . . AND THE BEST

—H. E. Y. S. AND J. Y.

FOR MY SWEET, FUNNY, QUIRKY, CREATIVE "BAD GIRL," VIVIAN

—R. G.

First paperback edition 2015
Text copyright © 2013 by Jane Yolen and Heidi E. Y. Stemple
Illustrations copyright © 2013 by Rebecca Guay
All rights reserved, including the right of reproduction in whole or in part in any form.
Charlesbridge and colophon are registered trademarks of Charlesbridge Publishing, Inc.

Published by Charlesbridge, 85 Main Street,Watertown, MA 02472
(617) 926-0329 • www.charlesbridge.com

Library of Congress Cataloging-in-Publication Data
Yolen, Jane.
    Bad girls: sirens, Jezebels, murderesses, thieves, and other female villains / Jane Yolen
and Heidi E. Y. Stemple; illustrated by Rebecca Guay.
       p. cm.
    Includes bibliographical references and index.
    ISBN 978-1-58089-185-1 (reinforced for library use)
    ISBN 978-1-58089-186-8 (softcover)
    ISBN 978-1-60734-538-1 (ebook)
    ISBN 978-1-60734-585-5 (ebook pdf)
1. Female offenders—Biography—Juvenile literature. 2. Femmes fatales—
Biography—Juvenile literature. 3. Women murderers—Biography—Juvenile literature.
I. Stemple, Heidi E. Y. II.Title.
CT3203.Y65 2012
364.3'740922—dc23
[B]   2012000783

Printed in China

(hc) 10 9 8 7 6 5 4 3 2
(sc) 10 9 8 7 6 5 4 3 2 1

Illustrations done in ink and brush on Bristol paper with digital color
Display type set in Populaire and text type set in Fairfield
Printed by 1010 Printing International Limited in Huizhou, Guangdong, China
Production supervision by Brian G. Walker
Designed by Susan Mallory Sherman

DOWNLOAD FREE EDUCATIONAL MATERIALS:
http://tinyurl.com/badgirlsreaderstheater
http://tinyurl.com/badgirlsdiscussion

TABLE OF CONTENTS

INTRODUCTION
BAD, MAD, OR THOROUGHLY ROTTEN 1

DELILAH (CIRCA 110 BCE)
A MERE SNIP OF A GIRL 5

JEZEBEL (9TH CENTURY BCE)
A PERFECTLY BAD QUEEN 11

CLEOPATRA (69-30 BCE)
THE QUEEN OF DENIAL 17

SALOME (CIRCA 14-71 CE)
A LITTLE STRIP OF A GIRL 25

ANNE BOLEYN (CIRCA 1500-1536)
SHE LOST HER HEAD FOR LOVE 31

BLOODY MARY (1516-1558)
A WOMAN OF BURNING FAITH 37

ELISABETH BÁTHORY (1560-1614)
COUNTESS BLOODBATH 43

MOLL CUTPURSE (CIRCA 1584-1659)
HIGH DIRECTRESS OF THE BLACK DOGS 47

TITUBA (CIRCA 1670s–?)

ONE WITCHY WOMAN 53

ANNE BONNEY (LATE 1600s–1720s)

AND MARY READ

PIRATES IN PETTICOATS 59

PEGGY SHIPPEN ARNOLD (1760–1804)

BRIDE OF TREASON 69

CATHERINE THE GREAT (1729–1796)

QUEEN OF COUPS 75

ROSE O'NEAL GREENHOW (1817–1864)

THE REBEL ROSE 81

BELLE STARR (1848–1889)

BELLE OF THE BAD-BOY BALL 85

CALAMITY JANE (CIRCA 1852–1903)

COURTIN' CALAMITY 91

LIZZIE BORDEN (1860–1927)

ONE WHACKY WOMAN 95

MADAME ALEXE POPOVA (1850s–1909)

SHE POPPED OVER THREE HUNDRED 101

PEARL HART (CIRCA 1871–1925)

MAMA'S WILD CHILD 105

TYPHOID MARY (1869–1938)

A COOK WITHOUT A CONSCIENCE 109

MATA HARI (1876–1917)

THE SPY WHO LOVED EVERYONE 115

MA BARKER (CIRCA 1873–1935)

MOTHER KNOWS WORST 121

BEULAH ANNAN (CIRCA 1901–1928)

AND BELVA GAERTNER (CIRCA 1885–1965)

CHICAGO'S MERRY MURDERESSES 127

BONNIE PARKER (1910–1934)

CLYDE'S GIRL 133

VIRGINIA HILL (1916–1966)

GANGSTER GIRLFRIEND 139

CONCLUSION

MODERN TIMES AND CHANGING GENDER ROLES . . . 145

BIBLIOGRAPHY 148

INDEX 158

AUTHOR AND ILLUSTRATOR BIOGRAPHIES 162

"WHEN I'M GOOD, I'M VERY GOOD. BUT WHEN I'M BAD, I'M BETTER."

—Mae West in *I'm No Angel*

BAD, MAD, OR THOROUGHLY ROTTEN

AN INTRODUCTION

THERE ARE MORE BAD GIRLS in history than we can count: murderesses, drunkards, torturers, batterers, fences, slatterns, liars, layabouts, and total louts, as well as wicked mothers, grandmothers, and stepmothers. The list is endless, even though females are supposedly the gentler sex.

Often, though, a tough girl, an outspoken girl—an active, smart, forward-looking girl—is mistaken for a bad one. A strong leader is considered a wrong leader when that leader is female.

In this book we are taking a look back through history at all manner of famous female felons. We're looking at the baddest of the bad, as well as those who may have been just misunderstood. The crimes in question happened hundreds, even thousands, of years ago—and some of them may have never happened at all. Our bad girls are a mixed bag. Some committed criminal acts, some morally wrong acts. Some acts are, perhaps, less criminal than justifiable, brave, or even committed in self-defense. We cannot compare badness by counting bodies. After all, do three hundred Protestants burned at the stake by Queen Mary outweigh the two that Lizzie Borden was accused (though acquitted) of killing? Nor can we compare badness by measuring crimes—Pearl Hart's stagecoach robbery might seem tame in comparison to Salome's hand in a great prophet's execution. Each bad girl can only be judged standing on her own.

Everyone is entitled to her own opinion, and you will see ours. We certainly don't always agree with each other, and we don't expect you to agree with us either. Every crime—no matter how heinous—comes with its own set of circumstances, aggravating and mitigating, which can tip the scales of guilt. And views change. The line between right and wrong, criminal and hero, good girl and bad, is sometimes very thin. Though some acts—and some girls—will always be bad through and through.

DELILAH

A MERE SNIP OF A GIRL

THE STRONGER A MAN, the harder he falls. Delilah was counting on it.

When Samson was born, his mother was so happy to have a baby that she promised an angel she would raise him as a Nazarite. Nazarites were people consecrated to God who never cut their hair. In exchange, the angel promised that Samson would have extraordinary powers and help deliver the Israelites from the hands of the Philistines who ruled them.

As Samson grew up and grew hair, he became as strong as the angel had promised. In one battle he single-handedly killed over a thousand Philistines using just the jawbone of a dead donkey. It was an astonishing feat. For the man and for the donkey.

Next Samson ripped the gate of Gaza from the ground and carried it on his shoulders while the Philistines fled. Samson led the Israelites for twenty years. He was the man.

Now the Philistines wanted Samson dead, but no man had the courage to face him. So of course they sent a woman to do the job.

That woman was Delilah. It is not known if she was a Philistine herself, but she was certainly in their pay. She was promised eleven hundred pieces of silver from each of the five Philistine chiefs to discover the source of Samson's strength.

Delilah was young, beautiful, smart—and sly. She put herself in Samson's way, and he fell for her. Hard. One day Delilah smiled her sexy smile, batted her sexy eyelashes, and said to Samson, "You are so strong. What makes you that way?"

Since he had promised his mother never to tell his secret, Samson lied. "Bind me with seven green bow-strings that have never been dried, and I will be as weak as any man."

While he slept, Delilah bound Samson with seven fresh bowstrings. Then she cried out, "Wake up, Samson, my love, the Philistines are here!" He woke, and snapped the bowstrings as if they were straw. So she knew he'd lied.

Delilah pouted. She wanted those pieces of silver. So she tried again. She smiled her sexy smile. She batted her sexy eyelashes. And Samson told her he could be weakened if bound with new ropes that had never been used. When he fell asleep, Delilah bound him again. He broke the ropes easily, too.

Delilah sulked. She swore Samson's lies were proof he didn't love her. But once again he lied, and once again she tried to weaken him while he slept. It didn't work.

After that, she would not stop nagging. Day and night Delilah complained. Night and day she whined. Until at last she threatened to leave if he lied to her again. So this time Samson told her the truth. It was his hair. Cut his hair, and he would be weak and wobbly and worthless. He would be wimpy and wilted and worn.

Delilah knew the truth when she heard it. When Samson fell back asleep, she had a servant come in and cut his hair and shave his beard. Then she called for the Philistines to bind Samson. He was caught. Delilah took her silver coins and left quickly.

Bound and weak, Samson was taken to a prison in Gaza, where his eyes were put out. The Philistines tied him to the pillars of their temple. Now bound, weak, and blind, he was left for everyone to see. Night after night, the Philistines were all so busy jeering at Samson and drinking wine, dancing, and partying that they didn't notice his hair had begun to grow again. As it grew, so did his strength. Finally, with that last bit of power, Samson tore the temple pillars down, killing himself and everyone inside.

But Delilah, the bad girl responsible for all that carnage, was long, long gone, along with her silver coins.

JEZEBEL

A PERFECTLY BAD QUEEN

JEZEBEL was a spoiled-rotten princess of biblical proportions. She was from Sidon, part of Phoenicia, which is now part of Lebanon. In Jezebel's time Sidon was a place where great parties and drunkenness were all the rage.

When Jezebel married Ahab, the king of straitlaced northern Israel, the spoiled-rotten princess became a spoiled-rotten queen.

The new queen never tried to fit in with her husband's people. She brought alien fertility gods like Baal and Astarte to her new home. She even persuaded her husband to build altars to worship them instead of Yahweh, the god of the Israelites. If you believed the gossip, her gods demanded the sacrifice of babies. And everyone believed the gossip. The people of northern Israel did not like their new queen.

Jezebel didn't stop there. She had many of the local Jewish priests and prophets persecuted and even killed for refusing to worship her gods. In their place she put 850 priests of Astarte and Baal.

King Ahab could not restrain his queen. In fact he didn't even try. Instead he followed where she led. And she gave him advice. Bad advice. *Very* bad advice.

When Ahab wanted to enlarge his lands by buying up his neighbor Naboth's property, Naboth refused, for it was the Jewish custom to keep land within a family. King Ahab went home to his queen to sulk. Jezebel found him on his bed, moaning, groaning, and refusing to eat.

While the king pouted, Jezebel sent messages to all the nobles and elders in the neighborhood to stone Naboth for cursing the king. She called it treason. After all, in Sidon, refusing the king's wishes was a crime punishable by death.

Unfortunately for poor Naboth, everyone did as Jezebel asked.

With Naboth dead, King Ahab claimed the lands for himself.

But no bad deed goes unpunished, and God himself sent the prophet Elijah to speak to King Ahab.

Dogs would eat the flesh of his queen, Elijah warned.

Harsh words.

Prophetic words.

But Ahab didn't live to see them come true. He died soon after Elijah's prophecy, and his son ascended to power. The new king tried but failed to win the hearts and minds of his people, and he was killed in a palace coup.

As for Jezebel, she may have been spoiled, but she was no dummy. She knew the end was near. Dressing in her finest gown, she darkened her eyes with kohl. Just because she was doomed was no reason to look bad. Glancing out the palace window, she saw an army riding toward her, led by the commander who had just killed her son.

"Throw the witch queen down!" cried the commander to the servants in the palace.

To save themselves, the servants pushed the queen out of the window to the streets below. There the army's horses trampled her to death.

The soldiers captured the palace and then went back to bury Jezebel—for though she was a bad queen, she was still a queen, and queens need grand, royal funerals and ornamental tombs.

But all the soldiers found were bits and pieces of her. Dogs had eaten the rest.

CLEOPATRA

THE QUEEN OF DENIAL

SEVENTEEN-YEAR-OLD CLEOPATRA married her ten-year-old brother, the future King Ptolemy XIII!

Though this sounds like a bad tabloid headline, it is not. It is history. Egyptian history.

The marriage was a plan cooked up by Ptolemy's three adult advisers, who wanted to rule all of Egypt by controlling the young couple. Unfortunately for the advisers, they underestimated Cleopatra. She may have been young, but she was no pushover.

Cleopatra wanted to make Egypt once again the jewel of the Nile, as it had been fourteen hundred years earlier. When she became queen, her first step was to strip her brother's advisers of the power they thought they deserved.

Did this make the advisers happy? Of course not. But they were wily men who'd long been in politics. They bided their time, and with Ptolemy's approval, they drove Cleopatra from her home, palace, and throne, setting her against her brother. Then they celebrated their victory.

They celebrated a little too soon. Cleopatra was not about to be denied her inheritance. An intelligent, seductive woman who spoke nine languages and had grown up in a family used to brutal politics, she raised an army of her own in Syria against her brother and his advisers.

But before Cleopatra could march against them, the famous Roman leader Julius Caesar arrived in Egypt. Caesar, the most powerful man of the most powerful nation in the known world, was set on having the Egyptian brother and sister make peace for the sake of the region. So he sent for the two of them.

Afraid that the beautiful Cleopatra could seduce even the great Caesar, Ptolemy's royal advisers ordered their soldiers to surround the palace where Caesar was staying.

The soldiers had orders to kill Cleopatra on sight,

but her spies warned her about the plan. Secretly she sailed into Alexandria's harbor in a small boat with a rug merchant. On Cleopatra's command, the merchant delivered a rug to Caesar's room at the palace.

This was probably the most desirable rug in the history of the world. In it, hidden from sight, was rolled the now twenty-two-year-old queen.

The advisers had been right to fear Cleopatra. Caesar fell completely in love with her. Though he was thirty years older and had a wife back in Rome, from that day on Caesar and Cleopatra lived together as husband and wife.

With Julius Caesar at her side, Cleopatra went to war. She ordered a siege of Ptolemy's palace. She had the drinking water poisoned. Her soldiers burned the Egyptian fleet. In one of the great battles for the throne, her brother-husband drowned in the Nile, his heavy golden armor pulling him down.

With her first brother-husband gone, Cleopatra shared her throne with another younger brother, Ptolemy XIV. But her love affair with Caesar continued. When he was called back to Rome, she joined him with their baby son, which certainly didn't please Caesar's wife, who also lived there.

In Rome Cleopatra had a lavish home and far too many servants. *This,* the people of Rome whispered, just wouldn't do. Everyone was afraid Caesar was going to set himself up as king, make Cleopatra his queen, and move the capital of the Roman Empire to Alexandria. *This,* whispered the Roman senators, just wouldn't do.

So they assassinated Caesar.

Cleopatra fled Rome with her young son, sailing back to Egypt.

Now Rome was to be ruled by three people, instead of just Julius Caesar: General Mark Antony, Marcus Lepidus, and Caesar's heir, Octavian. They divided up the Roman territories. Mark Antony got the eastern provinces, which included Egypt.

Marc Antony decided to visit his new lands and ordered Cleopatra to meet him.

Taking her time because she didn't like being ordered around, Cleopatra sailed out on a barge with purple sails and silver oars, the rowers accompanied by lutes and pipes. Cleopatra was dressed as the goddess of love, Venus, and lay under a golden canopy. Not surprisingly, Antony, too, fell instantly in love with her.

Antony and Cleopatra had three children and lived together in Alexandria, where Antony also fell in love with Alexandria's rich life, much grander than anything in Rome. He divorced his Roman wife, who was Octavian's sister, and gave Cleopatra a large part of Rome's eastern provinces as a gift.

Was Rome happy about this? No.

Was Octavian happy about this? No.

In fact, everybody was furious. With the support of the Roman people, Octavian declared war— not on Antony, but on Cleopatra.

The war raged for months. Many men were killed, and at last Octavian's ships blockaded the Egyptian fleet.

Cleopatra escaped back to Egypt on her private, treasure-laden ships. Antony followed her.

Back in Egypt Antony fell into a deep depression. He even tried to kill himself with his sword. But though he wounded himself severely, he did not die at once. Instead he lingered for a long while before finally succumbing to his wounds in his beloved Cleopatra's arms. She had him buried as a king.

Cleopatra was not going to go out like that. Poison, she thought, was the way to go. After testing all sorts of poisons on prisoners, she had an asp—a poisonous snake whose bite killed quickly—brought to her. And so the last queen of Egypt died as she had lived—by her own rules.

SALOME

A LITTLE STRIP OF A GIRL

SEXY SALOME stripped. One . . . two . . . three . . . four . . . five . . . six . . . seven. Slowly she dropped the seven veils that covered her. And though she was barely a teenager, sexy Salome knew just what she was doing.

Rome was filled with rabble. In this case, the rabble consisted of the local Jews. And the rabble was talking.

The rabble was talking about Salome's stepfather, Herod Antipas, the Roman governor-king of Galilee. He was cruel and unsavory.

The rabble was talking about Salome's mother, Herodias, who had left her husband to marry his half-brother, who was also her uncle—a real family affair! Such a marriage was illegal, the rabble mumbled.

Immoral, the people rumbled. Just plain icky, they jeered.

And the loudest of all the rabble was a raggedy preacher known as John the Baptist, who shouted his angry sermons in the public marketplace.

Herod Antipas was not amused. Who was this scraggly, homeless ranter? How dare the man speak that way about the governor's wife? Herod Antipas threw John the Baptist into prison in the great fortress of Machaerus.

Herod Antipas was not, however, ready to kill John the Baptist. He only wanted to shut him up. If John the Baptist was killed, he would become a martyr. Rabble without a cause is just rabble. But give that rabble a cause—a martyr—and it can quickly turn into a mob. And Herod Antipas knew that the Romans would not be happy with a mob on their hands.

Herodias had no such qualms. She'd been insulted in the marketplace, and she wanted John the Baptist dead. So she made a plan—one that would use Salome's youthful beauty as bait.

And what better place to extract revenge than at a party? Herod Antipas loved parties.

Herodias waited until Herod Antipas's birthday feast,

when all the important men of Galilee were assembled in the dining hall. After the men were full of food and alcohol, Herodias summoned Salome—who was a great favorite at court—and sent her out to dance before the men.

Dropping the seven veils that covered her, sexy Salome stripped. And she stripped well. Well enough to impress her stepfather.

Calling Salome to him, Herod Antipas promised—loudly enough that everyone in the room could hear—that he would give her anything she wanted as a reward for her wonderful dance.

This was a big decision. Salome was good at dancing, but not so good at knowing what to ask for. She went over to her mother and begged for advice.

Herod Antipas probably expected the girl to ask for diamonds, scarves, or a new slave. Perhaps even a pair of jeweled shoes. Those girly gifts might have been fine for young Salome, but they certainly weren't what her mother had in mind.

Herodias wanted something much different. And she told Salome to ask for it.

"I want you to give me the head of John the Baptist on a platter," Salome said. "Right now."

Herod Antipas had no choice but to give her what she asked for. He sent for the executioner.

Within the hour John the Baptist's head was brought to Salome on a silver salver. She carried the grisly reward proudly and set it before her mother, who only smiled.

ANNE BOLEYN

SHE LOST HER HEAD FOR LOVE

HENRY VIII of England was married to Queen Catherine when he fell in love. Oh, not with his queen. That would have been too simple. He fell in love with a graceful, black-eyed, dark-haired woman almost ten years his junior named Anne Boleyn.

The people who hated her—and there were many—believed Anne Boleyn was a witch who had enchanted their king. Their proof? She supposedly had six fingers on her left hand and a variety of moles on her body. They also said she had ruined the king and the queen and the Catholic Church. They were partly right.

At least she wasn't a witch.

Anne was the daughter of Thomas Boleyn, a remarkable man from whom Anne inherited a talent for languages. She was a very smart girl.

Thomas Boleyn arranged for Anne to be educated at

court so she would learn to read and write at a time when few women not of the royal family could do so. She was being trained to marry well. Perhaps even to meet King Henry? Well, a pretty girl, a smart girl who was already part of the aristocracy, might become a favorite of the king's. From there her good marriage would be assured. It was a game most of the best families played.

Before this happened, however, Anne Boleyn fell in love with a boy her own age, the rich Lord Percy. They promised to marry one another even though marriages at the time were arranged for reasons of power, not love. The two lovebirds may have married secretly, but if they did, they kept it quiet.

But then young Anne met King Henry. He was thirty-five and married to a queen he liked but did not love. He needed a son as heir to the Tudor throne. Queen Catherine had given Henry a daughter but was now too old to have any more children.

Suddenly a black-eyed, dark-haired, sharp-tongued, bold young woman appeared in court as the queen's newest lady-in-waiting. Smitten, King Henry wrote to Anne in 1526 that he was "struck with the dart of love," and he meant it.

By May 1527 the king had made up his mind. He

wanted to marry Anne. But he was already married. And he was Catholic. All of England was Catholic. Catholics—even Catholic kings—were not allowed to divorce. So as a last resort, lovesick King Henry dissolved the British Catholic Church, set himself up as supreme head of his own religion—the Church of England, a form of Protestantism—and divorced his wife.

What did Anne Boleyn do to encourage this? Everything she could. She told the king she was unmarried and a virgin who would bear him sons. She encouraged him to declare his daughter Mary illegitimate. She sang and danced with him. She rode out hunting with him. She wrote poems to him. And the king was so besotted that anyone who spoke a bad word about Anne was immediately thrown into prison.

Anne did not complain. She teased him, flattered him, made all kinds of promises, and at last, in January 1533, just days after his divorce, she married him. She was crowned queen five months later.

When she gave birth to the child she'd been sure would be a son, no one was more surprised than she that the baby was a girl. That girl, Elizabeth, would one day become the greatest queen of England. But

Anne Boleyn would never live to see her daughter reign.

Henry, of course, still wanted a son. So Anne got pregnant again, and quickly. This baby was born dead. The unhappy king was surrounded by beautiful young women vying for his attention. Eventually he turned that attention to Jane Seymour. The *really* unhappy Queen Anne got pregnant for a third time, but she miscarried again, a boy child.

As Jane Seymour received more and more of the king's attention, the new queen raged at her husband. King Henry did not take her rages lightly. It was the beginning of the end for Anne Boleyn.

King Henry had already divorced one wife. Queen Anne he treated even more cruelly. On trumped-up charges that she had had love affairs with many men, including her own brother, she was imprisoned in the Tower of London, where it was said that she plotted the king's murder. Wouldn't you?

That's where Queen Anne Boleyn lost her head. Literally. The day after she was beheaded, Henry engaged himself to Jane Seymour, and they were married less than a month later. And after that, no one—*no one*—had anything nice to say about Anne Boleyn.

BLOODY MARY

A WOMAN OF BURNING FAITH

LEADING A VERY PUBLIC LIFE can be injurious to your health. And to others'. Princess Mary Tudor found this out when her father, King Henry VIII (yes, *that* King Henry), left her mother, Queen Catherine, so he could marry a pretty girl named Anne (yes, *that* Anne). Henry wanted a son to inherit his kingdom, and Queen Catherine was well past her childbearing years.

This was bad enough, but the king had also divorced his wife and then, for good measure, declared the marriage annulled, which meant legally it had never happened. Now Mary was considered an illegitimate child—no longer Princess Mary but Lady Mary—and could never rule England.

Mary was no soft princess kept in an ivory tower.

She was well educated, spoke several languages, had a lovely singing voice, and was already sought in marriage by European princes and kings. But she hated her father for what he had done to her mother, and even more for setting aside the Catholic religion and making himself the head of the new English faith. She hated his new wife, too, who had once been her mother's lady-in-waiting and who now had Henry's love *and* Catherine's jewelry! And Mary hated the red-headed baby Elizabeth perhaps the most, because little Elizabeth was now Henry's adored princess and heir to the throne.

To make sure Mary could not stir up trouble with all her hatreds, Henry sent her away from court. She was denied any communication with her beloved mother. During this time, Mary got sick. Terribly sick—headaches, nausea, insomnia, the lot.

Hearing that his eldest daughter was ill, the king relented. Sort of. He offered her a pardon and a promise to restore her to favor, but only if she would acknowledge him as head of the new church. At first she refused, but eventually, grudgingly, she gave in.

As if things weren't bad enough, Mary's mother died, and Mary had to live away from court to wait upon her own half sister, baby Elizabeth, heir to Mary's rightful crown.

But then everything changed. The hated Anne Boleyn was executed. The new queen—meek Jane Seymour—encouraged Henry to reunite with Mary. So Mary was brought back to court and became a friend to the new queen. She was even named god-mother to the new baby, Prince Edward. Yes, a boy was born to King Henry at last. Sadly for Mary, Queen Jane died less than two weeks after her son's birth, so it was a short friendship.

King Henry married three more times, but none of his marriages was very successful. When Henry finally died, nine-year-old Edward became king. But not only was he young, he was sickly. And stubborn. He enforced English Protestantism, which forced Mary to continue practicing her Catholic faith in secret. When Edward died at fifteen, Mary's cousin Lady Jane Grey took the throne. That lasted nine whole days.

Only now did Mary make her move. She rode to London with an army of her supporters, and the people welcomed her with great affection. She took the throne herself and had Lady Jane and her husband arrested, tried, and eventually beheaded, along with their fathers. Mary was back where she belonged, with a vengeance.

After that, Queen Mary brought back the Catholic faith to England. She enforced the old heresy laws, executing anyone not practicing Catholicism. In fact, during her reign Mary had three hundred people burned at the stake, earning her the nickname Bloody Mary. It was said that the stench of the burnings covered London for months.

Of course, Mary needed an heir, so at age thirty-eight she married Prince Philip II of Spain, another Catholic monarch, who up until then had been considered a great enemy of England. If the burning of heretics had earned her enemies throughout England, this marriage did little to help her gain supporters.

But Mary never had the child she needed, and her Spanish husband went back to his own country. She was forced to name Elizabeth, the sister she had never liked, as her heir. After just five bloody years on the throne, Mary died. Few mourned her.

ELISABETH BÁTHORY

COUNTESS BLOODBATH

NOT WANTING TO HAVE wrinkles and gray hair is normal. Bathing in human blood to prevent them is something else altogether.

One of the most heinous murderers of all time—man or woman—was the countess Elisabeth Báthory. The sheer number of her victims found dead and dying—perhaps more than five hundred—is enough to put her in the running for the world title. The reasons for her murderous spree? Vanity and boredom.

Elisabeth Báthory was the daughter of a Hungarian baron. When still a child, she was shipped off to marry a count. But soon after the wedding, her husband left her in their castle in northwestern Hungary and rode off to fight in one of the many European wars. So Elisabeth was bored. Witchcraft and magic became the pale-skinned, dark-haired beauty's new hobbies.

The witchcraft she enjoyed had nothing to do with broomsticks and black cats. And the magic? Well, let's just say she wasn't pulling any bunnies out of a hat.

The countess was fond of all sorts of horrible acts, but it wasn't until after her husband died—she was forty-four—that she really started dabbling in *black* magic. Soon girls and young women in the area started disappearing. *The countess wants their blood,* the rumors said. *To bathe in! To make her young!*

Those rumors spread all the way to the king of Hungary, but it took him years to get around to stopping her. After all, one of Elisabeth's cousins was prime minister and another was governor. When the king's soldiers finally put an end to the countess's reign of terror, they found hundreds of dead and dying in her basement dungeon. It was gruesome beyond description.

Elisabeth's accomplices and the servants who aided her in her quest for blood were sentenced to horrible deaths, but Elisabeth, because she was an important person from a good family, was locked in her bedroom.

Since even a countess can't cheat old age and death forever, four years later, still under house arrest, Elisabeth Báthory died quietly, all alone, in her room.

MOLL CUTPURSE

HIGH DIRECTRESS OF
THE BLACK DOGS

IF YOU'RE GOING TO PLAY with the big bad boys, you can't be named Mary Frith. You can't be the daughter of an honest shoemaker. You have to call yourself something bigger and badder, which is how Mary Frith became Moll Cutpurse.

Mary was born in London in the 1580s with both fists clenched, which was thought to be a sure sign of a wild and adventurous spirit. She was called in her time a *tomrig,* which is a rude, wild, wanton girl. She was also a *rumpscuttle,* a girl who had little regard for the traditional feminine pursuits. In other words, she was a complete tomboy. She beat up all the boys on the block. Later she mastered sword fighting and won many duels. She ran away to the

Bear Garden to watch the bearbaiting, a contest in which a bear tied to a stake battled a pack of dogs.

Mary was a handful, all right. She was loud and assertive. She cursed like a sailor. She was certainly not marriageable. So her family put her on a ship bound for Virginia to be sold there to a plantation owner as a bond servant.

But Mary jumped ship before it ever left port, changed her name to Moll, and made her way into the London underworld, pretending for a time to be a young man.

She quickly became part of a gang of thieves who did their business around the popular London-area resort towns. She was good at slitting pockets and extracting purses, but better still at planning robberies and disposing of the stolen merchandise.

Her gang did so well that anyone finding themselves short of a purse or missing a watch or a picket of coins came immediately to Moll's door on Fleet Street to try to reclaim their possessions.

Her new name? Moll Cutpurse. Her job description? Ransoming stolen goods for a set price.

Her job title? Black Dog.

Moll Cutpurse became the best-known Black Dog

in all of London. Her fellow Black Dogs called her the High Directress of Crime. Highwaymen who were too well known to sell their ill-gotten gains brought their loot to Moll's house, knowing she wouldn't cheat them.

Moll was soon famous. Authors wrote about her. People talked about her. She was a familiar sight at the Devil's Tavern in her men's clothing. Moll frowned on violence, except for her bearbaiting dogs, each of which had its own bed in her house. And for the most part, she obeyed the laws of the kingdom, since fencing stolen goods was legal back then. Like a modern-day celebrity, she was followed around by admirers who treated her to her favorite drinks. She was the first woman in London to smoke tobacco, or so she claimed. Often she had well-known writers and adventurers to her house for parties. And the High Directress's house? Always immaculate.

Moll Cutpurse prospered for many years—until the king of England, Charles I, was executed by Oliver Cromwell's Puritan party. The British Civil War began, and new laws against such things as fencing stolen goods all but drove Moll out of business.

Moll was getting on in years, but she went back to

robbery and continued to thrive. She also put aside twenty pounds of her enormous fortune to celebrate with when the British kings were restored to power. Alas, she died of dropsy a year before that happened, and never got to lift a tankard to King Charles II.

TITUBA

ONE WITCHY WOMAN

THE PURITANS were not fun people. Their children had no fun, either. In fact, having fun was pretty much against their religion and therefore against their laws. So what was a Puritan girl to do?

If you were Betty Parris or Abigail Williams, you would have your slave, Tituba, entertain you with fantastic stories of magic from the plantation on Barbados where she'd lived as a child. Now *those* were great stories.

Tituba had been born in South America, but early on she had been sold as a slave. Eventually she was bought by a Puritan named Samuel Parris and brought to New England.

When Parris became the pastor of Salem Village in 1689, Tituba became caretaker to the Parris children—Betty and her siblings, Thomas and Susanna—as well as their cousin Abigail.

Like all Puritan children, the Parris children were expected to help with the cooking and the cleaning, the candle making, butter churning, and wheat threshing. That's a *lot* of chores. This left little time for mischief.

But even Puritan children could find trouble.

The girls began playing fortune-telling games, like cracking eggs into water so the floating shapes could be read to tell the future.

If Tituba knew about these games, she probably paid them no mind. After all, in New England most everyone did this. They just did it quietly, out of the minister's sight.

As for Tituba, she *said* she knew real magic. She *said* that her mistress on Barbados had been a witch. She said. . . . She said. . . .

Oh, the stories Tituba told the children, stories about fantastic spells and voodoo—all odd rituals from a world alien to the girls.

So when the girls began acting in strange ways— *really* strange ways—convulsing, complaining of pains, shouting, twitching, hallucinating, crawling around on the ground, and having trouble breathing, the people of Salem Village pointed accusing fingers at the foreigner, the witch, Tituba.

First, though, they asked for her help. One such request came from Mary Sibley, a village woman. She asked Tituba to bake a witch cake, a disgusting recipe that included urine as an ingredient. They fed this cake to the family dog. This was supposed to reveal who was bewitching the girls.

It didn't.

What it did was get Tituba into trouble. Big trouble.

The girls claimed she was a witch. Reverend Parris beat her badly and ordered her to confess. The village people were all too happy to have someone to put on trial.

And so, to save her life, Tituba confessed.

She said she flew on a pole.

She said she saw visions.

She said she'd signed the devil's book.

There was a trial, and Tituba was jailed. Lucky for her, she was spared hanging—though many in Salem were not—because in Puritan New England, a confession would save you from the gallows. Nevertheless, she remained in jail even after she and all the other confessed "witches" of Salem were pardoned, because her master, Reverend Parris, refused to pay her jail costs.

Finally Tituba was sold to another family and was never heard from again.

ANNE BONNEY AND MARY READ

PIRATES IN PETTICOATS

ANNE BONNEY

"If you had fought like a man you need not be hang'd like a dog." So said Anne Bonney to her lover, Captain "Calico Jack" Rackham. They were both in prison for their pirate misdeeds.

And she was right. On board their sloop, *Vanity*, Rackham and his crew had been too busy drinking and playing cards to fight when the governor's ship came to capture them. Only two had remained on deck ready to fight: Anne Bonney and her best friend, Mary Read.

The story of Anne Bonney begins in Ireland around 1697, when a handsome married lawyer eloped to the Carolinas with a pregnant serving girl. There the new mother died when her daughter was still small, so baby Anne grew up motherless, headstrong, and willful. When she stabbed the cook during an argument about a chicken dinner, her father said the woman "was in her time a pretty good cook, but she was a bit opinionated and my daughter is to be excused for losing her temper."

Much to her doting father's dismay, Anne ran off with an ex-pirate named James Bonney. Her father warned that he would disinherit her if she married Bonney.

She did—and he did.

Totally broke, the newlyweds moved to Nassau, where Anne wanted to join a pirate crew. But Bonney thought spying on his ex-comrades would be more profitable. Disgusted by this, Anne ran off with the colorful pirate Calico Jack Rackham. Bonney did not like this at all. So with the governor's help, he dragged Anne back and threatened her with a public whipping.

Just as Anne's father had learned that threats didn't

work on Anne, so did Bonney. Dressed in a pair of striped seamen's trousers, with a cutlass and two pistols by her side and her long hair tucked under a hat, Anne sneaked out to meet Rackham and eight of his men. They renamed the disguised Anne Tom Bonney, and the ten of them stole the sloop *Vanity*. Anne was finally a pirate.

MARY READ

Before Mary Read was born, her grandmother promised a sizeable fortune should she be given a grandson. Instead all she got was Mary. So Mary's mother did what any mother in this situation might do: she dressed little Mary as a boy in an attempt to fool her rich mother-in-law. But it seems the old lady figured out the scam, because when she died, Mary got nothing.

Calling Mary "Buttons," her mother apprenticed her as a footboy, helping the footmen on the carriages of fine ladies. Still disguised as a boy, Mary ran off to sea to become a powder monkey, carrying explosives to the guns on board a warship. Next she enlisted as a soldier, but then ran off to join the cavalry. Mary craved excitement.

As a soldier, Mary fell in love with her tent mate. When she told him she was really a woman, they were quickly married and left the army to set up a popular inn near the army garrison.

Who knows which Mary would have tired of first—the inn or her husband. But he died of a fever, and then peace broke out. The garrison closed, and the inn went broke. The choice was made for Mary. She had neither husband nor job left. So, dressed as a man once again and calling herself James Morris, she ran off to sea.

When her ship was captured by English pirates, Mary joined them. She loved being a pirate. But she was used to doing things the legal way, so she jumped ship and joined a privateering crew, attacking enemy ships in the name of the king. This way she could have the adventures of a pirate legally.

Alas for Mary, two weeks later the privateers voted to become pirates themselves, so they could keep all their ill-gotten gains rather than share them with the government. In one of their first raids, a quiet sailor was brought on board. Mary fell in love again.

When the quartermaster of their ship planned a

duel with her sailor love, Mary picked a fight with the quartermaster and scheduled it before the men's fight. The quartermaster laughed and called her womanish. Little did he know.

They fought their duel ashore, and Mary shot the quartermaster. Before he died, she bared her breast and said, "You called me a woman and struck me on the cheek. Well! It is in truth a woman who kills you that she may teach others to respect her."

Back on board, she and the quiet sailor planned to marry. They snuck off and shipped out with Rackham and his crew aboard *Vanity*.

TOGETHER

On *Vanity*, Anne (as Tom Bonney) and Mary (as James Morris) became fast friends. The crew knew that Tom Bonney was really Rackham's wife. They respected her because she was as rough and tough as any of them. And *she* probably knew that James Morris was Mary Read. But Rackham didn't know. In fact, he feared that the new tall, handsome sailor had stolen his wife's heart. To put Rackham at ease, Mary gave up her disguise. After that, the two women sometimes wore women's clothing on board, but in battle they dressed in men's jackets and long trousers, with kerchiefs tied about their heads. It was simply easier to fight that way.

The addition to the crew came just in time. The *Vanity* had been "at low game" with so few pirates on board. Anne had left the ship to have a baby and was just newly back. Understaffed, the only pirating the *Vanity* crew had done was to attack small ships and a couple of cattle farms on Haiti. However, now that they had a full crew, they captured a large schooner belonging to Captain James Spenlow. Suddenly the pirates found themselves in possession of not only the fine ship and its rigging, but also fifty rolls of tobacco and nine bags of pimentos, prizes that would bring them much-needed cash.

It was their biggest haul of the year—and their biggest mistake. As soon as he was released, Spenlow went right to Governor Woods Rogers. He described Rackham's ship and crew. Rogers immediately sent the man-of-war *Albion* and its crew of forty-five men to find *Vanity*. When they rounded the westernmost point of Jamaica, they spotted the sloop.

Quietly *Albion* crept up on Rackham's ship. To

Captain Barnet's surprise, there were only two men on deck. What Barnet didn't know was that the two were not men at all. They were Anne Bonney and Mary Read. The rest of the crew was below, drinking stolen rum. The women pirates called down the hatch for help.

The drunken men laughed up at them. Furious, Anne fired a blast down the hatch, killing one pirate and injuring several others. Then, standing shoulder-to-shoulder, armed to the teeth with pistols and cutlasses, Anne and Mary prepared to bravely battle the man-of-war and its forty-five heavily armed sailors by themselves.

The women fought valiantly but were quickly over-powered. Two against forty-five is not a fair fight. All the pirates were rounded up and brought to trial. Anne was allowed to visit Jack in prison, and it was there she told him he'd be hanged like a dog.

And they all *were* hanged. The men, that is. But when Anne and Mary faced the judge, they told him, "My lord, we plead our bellies." Their big pregnant bellies. They knew no judge would hang them, because that would have meant murdering the innocent children they were carrying.

What happened after that? No one is sure. Rumor

said they gave birth and were let go. Or died in jail. But perhaps both quietly dressed as men and set sail on another pirate adventure to plunder and fight and fall in love again out on the seven seas.

Peggy Shippen Arnold

PEGGY SHIPPEN ARNOLD

BRIDE OF TREASON

BENEDICT ARNOLD should have stayed a widower. But instead the military commander of Philadelphia married the very young, very beautiful, blonde, gray-eyed Peggy Shippen. She came from a proud family of Tories. Her father, a well-known judge, was still loyal to the British king some three years into the American War for Independence.

Benedict Arnold should have stayed a widower. Though not a rich man, he managed to find enough money to put a down payment on a magnificent ninety-six-acre estate called Mount Pleasant. Judge Shippen gave his begrudging consent, and the two were married.

Newly married Peggy was determined to live as she

had before that pesky war interfered. She had a plan. Secretly loyal to the British—even though now married to a hero of the Revolution—Peggy was probably already in the pay of the British. She almost certainly wrote coded messages about the American armies to her friend and ex-suitor Major John André, now aide to the British commander in chief.

While Peggy schemed and spied, Arnold was making his own plans to better their fortunes. In fact, he got caught misusing government wagons and issuing an improper pass to a ship while collecting a bribe. He was court-martialed. So much for being a hero.

So Peggy took over. She had Arnold write to André, proposing himself as a spy. Arnold's offer was one the British couldn't refuse. After all, Arnold was a high-ranking officer, a genuine hero—never mind the court-martial. Peggy was delighted when his offer was accepted.

In 1780 Arnold was able to persuade General George Washington to give him command of West Point, a key fort overlooking the Hudson River north of New York City. Unbeknownst to Washington, Arnold intended to hand the fort over to the British for a purse of twenty thousand pounds, a fortune in those days. Arnold also sent the British a complete itinerary for Washington's trip to Hartford, Connecticut.

Unfortunately for Arnold, Major André was captured while carrying the information in his socks. When he heard of André's capture, Arnold knew his own treachery would soon be discovered. He fled West Point, telling Peggy that he must leave her and his country forever. Then he boarded a British ship and sailed to New York and relative safety until he could find passage across the ocean to Britain.

Peggy was left behind with their baby. Time to make more plans.

Soon after, Washington came to visit to tell her what had befallen her traitor husband. Peggy gave the performance of her life. Pointing to the general, she cried out, "That is not General Washington! That is the man who was a-going to kill my baby!" She acted the madwoman for hours.

Washington and his officers were so affected by the sight of this poor, raving, innocent woman driven mad by her husband's deeds that they issued her a pass to travel back to her parents in Philadelphia. She left as soon as she could.

Once in Philadelphia, Peggy quickly recovered her

sanity. Staying at the home of a British colonel, she bragged to a friend about how she'd fooled Washington and all his men.

A year later, Peggy got on a ship and joined her husband in London, where—it's said—she received a pension from the British government for all the good work she had done for them.

CATHERINE THE GREAT

QUEEN OF COUPS

SOPHIE FRIEDERIKE AUGUSTE von Anhalt-Zerbst (nicknamed Figchen) was a minor German princess with a major desire to become a queen. Any queen. Of any country.

So when fifteen-year-old Figchen got the chance to marry Peter, the future tsar of Russia, she was ready, willing, and more than able. And since he was not a man of strong character, Peter was perfect. Figchen knew she could rule him, and therefore his country.

First she worked hard at learning the Russian language, walking barefoot about her drafty bedroom at night, repeating her lessons. She overdid it and came down with a nasty case of pneumonia. It did nothing to slow her down. Figchen was on a mission.

Then she converted to the Russian Orthodox religion in order to be accepted in Russia. She would do anything to become queen. Even change her name. Gone was Figchen. Renamed Catherine Alexeyevna, she married her Prince Not-So-Charming a year later.

Their honeymoon, however, was short-lived.

The marriage turned sour almost immediately. Peter, who was a year older than Catherine, was totally uninterested in his wife. He preferred his toy soldiers and dolls. Peter was one dull dolt of a tsar.

Catherine kept busy by continuing her education, learning about current events all over Russia and Europe and corresponding with such great writer-philosophers as Voltaire and Diderot. And she had boyfriends on the side. A girl can't study *all* the time!

Catherine had two sons. Neither of them was fathered by the tsar. He was too busy with his toy soldiers and dolls to care.

After Catherine and Peter had been unhappily married for seventeen years, his aunt died and he was placed on the Russian throne as Peter III. Catherine finally got what she'd always wanted—she was a queen.

Peter was as bad a tsar as he was a husband, and

soon he was hated within Russia as well as without. Six months after Peter became tsar, he took a vacation with all of his courtiers. He left his wife behind. It was a particularly stupid move by a particularly stupid man.

The palace guards revolted and put Catherine on the throne in his place. She did not discourage this. In fact, it was pretty clear that she arranged it. No blood was shed in this palace coup. But Catherine more than made up for that in the years to come.

A few short days later, the ousted tsar was killed in an "accident." The killer? The brother of Catherine's current boyfriend. Coincidence? No one knows for sure. Soon after, two other imprisoned contenders for the Russian throne also died: Ivan VI murdered, and Princess Tarakanova dead of tuberculosis. Coincidence? Probably not.

She may have been called Catherine the Great, but she could have been called Catherine the Ruthless, for she was never afraid to fight dirty. She ruled with a heavy hand. Yes, she did great things for Russia— modernizing agriculture, education, mining, medicine, and the fur trade. But she did ruthless things as well— starting wars with her neighbors and placing her old lovers on the thrones of friendly states. She did such things in equal measure until her death thirty-four years later.

She died as Catherine of Russia. Figchen was long forgotten.

ROSE O'NEAL GREENHOW

THE REBEL ROSE

ROSE O'NEAL GREENHOW knew how to throw a party. She invited only the most interesting and influential guests. The conversation was always stimulating, the food always perfect. But the hostess with the mostest had an ulterior motive. Rose was a passionate secessionist and a spy for the Confederacy during the American Civil War. Any important dinner conversation between her Union guests at her Washington DC home was quickly passed on to the Confederates.

The Maryland-born widow of a State Department official had many friends in Washington. But when the war broke out in 1861, Rose acted upon her Southern loyalty by sending a young woman dressed as a poor country girl to General Beauregard, a Confederate. Hidden in the girl's hair was a coded note about the Union troops' next attack. Because of Rose's information, Beauregard was able to defend the South at Bull Run.

After a search of Rose's house revealed her secret life as a spy, "Rebel Rose" was held under house arrest. But she did not quit spying. She kept listening and smuggling information to her Confederate friends. After getting caught again, she was sent to prison with her eight-year-old daughter. This just made her more of a Confederate hero. When she was tried in court, Southern tempers got hotter.

Finally, in order to calm the brewing Confederate anger, Rose was freed and sent south, under the judge's orders not to return during the course of the war. Rose was welcomed as a hero and was soon sent on a trip overseas to drum up British aid for the South. She spent a year schmoozing with British bigwigs, including the queen. On her return from this mission, the boat carrying her ran aground off the coast of North Carolina, which was being blockaded by Union troops. Fearing recapture, she tried to escape in a rowboat. Unfortunately, the rowboat capsized and the Rebel Rose—thorn in the Union's side—drowned.

BELLE STARR

BELLE OF THE BAD-BOY BALL

BELLE STARR was not born bad; in fact, she was born Myra Maybelle Shirley. But it didn't take bad long to find this well-educated Missouri girl.

And bad was wearing cowboy boots.

When the Civil War broke out, Belle got her kicks spying on the position of Union troops and reporting to the Confederacy. She sent her information through her brother Bud, who rode with the dreaded Quantrill's Raiders, a group of pro-Confederacy guerilla fighters from the South.

But Belle's beloved Bud was killed, and the family's fortunes were ruined. Belle and her family moved to

Texas to rebuild their lives. In Texas, the Shirley house became a haven for the defeated Rebels.

One of the many bad guys who visited the Shirley house was Jim Reed. Belle fell in love and married Reed, and it didn't matter that he became a horse thief, a counterfeiter, and a robber. He was just the kind of man Belle liked. Bad.

The couple had two children. But after Reed's death at the hands of the law, Belle dropped them off with relatives and married a Cherokee bad boy named Sam Starr. Starr and Belle ran quite a business, stealing horses, rustling cattle, and selling bootleg liquor. They harbored fugitive outlaws at their home. It was a good life for a bad couple—until Starr got thrown in jail.

What Belle couldn't get with her ill-gotten wealth, she could always get by flirting. But her charms didn't work on Judge Isaac Parker. He was determined to bring her to justice. He had very little luck until she was caught red-handed stealing horses.

Finally he put her in jail. But upon her release she fell right back into her life of crime.

The stories of Belle Starr, the Bandit Queen, were

always larger than life. They said that she rode down the streets shooting off her guns. That she dressed as a man when committing robberies. That she had appealed to the White House itself to help an imprisoned friend, relative, or lover.

Some of the stories had a kernel of truth in them, but most were exaggerated by papers such as the *National Police Gazette.* While these stories made her out to be glamorous, she was once described as "bony and flat-chested with a mean mouth; hatchet faced; a gotch-toothed tart." Not an attractive description!

Both her children—Pearl and Eddie—took up lives of crime as well. After all, what else did either of them know?

Eventually Sam Starr was let out of jail on bail and died in a gunfight. Not one to be alone for long, Belle was linked with other outlaws, including her third husband, Jim July. But that marriage ended abruptly when Belle was shot in the back. Likely the shooter was one of her bad men—her husband, her son, or an outlaw named Edgar Watson, all of whom Belle had been feuding with.

It didn't matter who shot her: Belle was dead, two days shy of her forty-first birthday.

On her tombstone is the following verse:

> *Shed not for her the bitter tear,*
> *Nor give the heart to vain regret.*
> *'Tis but the casket that lies here,*
> *The gem that filled it sparkles yet.*

CALAMITY JANE

COURTIN' CALAMITY

MARTHA JANE'S life was a calamity. Her mother died when Martha Jane was young. Her father and brothers were separated from her in an Indian uprising, and she had to fend for herself. Or maybe it was that both her parents died when she was eighteen. Who could tell? Martha Jane Cannary almost never told the truth.

She learned to shoot and ride early in life. By twenty she was an army scout. She wore men's clothing and smoked a cigar. In Wyoming she rode into a fight between some Indians and a small contingent of soldiers. There she picked up the fallen Captain Egan and saved him by riding off with him across her saddle. The rest of the soldiers were slaughtered.

When Egan recovered, he nicknamed his rescuer Calamity Jane. Or so the story goes. But if Calamity Jane told it, then maybe it was a lie.

The *St. Paul Dispatch* wrote: "She got her name from a faculty she has had of producing a ruction at any time and place and on short notice."

Wherever the truth lay, if a man offended her, she said he was "courtin' calamity." And many men tried to do just that. Court her, that is. She was a pretty, blue-eyed young woman, after all.

She was also an Indian killer from her days as a scout. A woman who dressed like a man. Who drank whiskey in bars with the men. Who swore like the toughest of mule-train drivers. Who considered herself "a daring and reckless rider."

Once she rescued a stagecoach full of passengers by leading a party of Plains Indians away from them. Afterward she circled back, took the reins from the hands of the dead driver, and drove the coach to its destination in Deadwood. Or so she said.

Eventually Calamity Jane joined Buffalo Bill's Wild West Show, where she remained until she retired, or was fired. You decide. Calamity Jane herself told both stories.

LIZZIE BORDEN

ONE WHACKY WOMAN

"Lizzie Borden took an ax,
gave her mother forty whacks.
When she saw what she had done,
gave her father forty-one!"

LIZZIE BORDEN didn't really whack her mother. Her mother died of a perfectly respectable disease when Lizzie was only two. The ax whacking occurred years later, in 1892, and the mother in question was Lizzie's *step*mother. And, really, it was only eighteen whacks. See how stories grow?

Lizzie and her sister, Emma, didn't much like their stepmother, Abby Borden. Their father, Andrew Borden, a wealthy but miserly bank president from Fall River,

Massachusetts, had married her in 1865, when Lizzie was five and Emma fourteen. Whether it was for love or because he needed someone to watch his girls, it didn't matter. This wasn't a happy family.

As the girls grew up, things got worse.

On Thursday, August 4, 1892, the Bordens began an ordinary day. Abby and Andrew Borden had been very sick two nights earlier, but they were feeling better. They joined Emma and the girls' uncle, John Morse, for breakfast. Lizzie stayed in bed and ate alone later. After Emma and Uncle John left for the day, first Abby Borden was killed—eighteen whacks with an ax in the spare bedroom—followed shortly thereafter by Andrew Borden—eleven whacks to the head on the sitting-room sofa.

Lizzie was pretty calm. Calling the maid downstairs, she announced, "Come down quick! Father's dead. Somebody's come in and killed him!"

There were plenty of suspects. Emma and Uncle John could have wanted the elder Bordens dead. The family *had* complained of a break-in earlier, so perhaps the burglar had returned and killed them. A rich man like Andrew Borden would have made enemies. Had someone tried to poison the family two days before?

One by one, suspects were cleared. No motive. Good alibi. No proof. All were cleared except the person who had found the bodies. Lizzie Borden.

Evidence started stacking up. There were two axes found in the Borden basement, and one had a missing handle. Lizzie had burned a stained dress shortly after the murders. Her alibi—that she had been in the barn—didn't hold up. There were no footprints there. It was common knowledge that Lizzie did not like her stepmother and was not happy with her father. She would inherit lots of money when they died. And Lizzie was cool. Not hysterical, as the good folks of Fall River thought she would be after half her family had been killed.

So they decided to put her on trial.

The trial of Lizzie Borden was big news. Evidence was presented. Some evidence seemed damning. A pharmacist claimed Lizzie had attempted to buy poison from him just before the elder Bordens became ill. Other evidence seemed to imply that Lizzie was innocent. The axes were coated with rust and cow's hair, not blood and human hair.

Lizzie's statements about the murders were inconsistent, her alibi illogical. No one could be found who had seen anyone entering or leaving the house the morning of the murders. In one gasp-inducing, theatrical courtroom moment, the ax from the Borden basement was fit into a hack mark on Andrew Borden's skull. It was a *perfect* fit.

But when it came down to it, the jury—possibly swayed as much by their perception that Lizzie was an upstanding, God-fearing, respected woman as by any legal evidence—pronounced her not guilty.

Lizzie returned home a rich woman. Her life, however, was not without drama after her acquittal. There were people who still thought she was guilty and never let her forget it. She and her sister, Emma, eventually had a falling-out, and Emma moved out of the home they'd bought with their inheritance.

Lizzie died mostly alone, with only her staff for company. She was buried next to her father in the family plot. Whether he would have approved, we will never know.

MADAME ALEXE POPOVA

SHE POPPED OVER THREE HUNDRED

IF YOUR MAN IS CRUEL and you want him gone, who ya gonna call? Popova.

Little news escaped from Russia in the early 1900s. Secrecy was a way of life. That's why hardly anything is known about Russia's most prolific poisoner. What is known is that Madame Alexe Popova had a bustling business that helped rid wives of troublesome husbands. At that time, if a Russian woman had a cruel, abusive, or just plain annoying husband, she didn't have a lot of options. She could suffer silently— or she could call on Madame Popova.

It was 1879 when Madame Popova opened her business. She didn't charge much and promised absolute Russian secrecy. Her method? Poison. Either she would give it to the unsuspecting husband herself or she would have someone on her "staff" do it. And she was good at it. Many Russian women were relieved of the burdens of matrimony in this way.

Madame Popova's business flourished. And the widows were merry. All but one. This newly widowed woman eventually started feeling bad. Bad because she had paid to have her husband killed. So she talked to the police.

Though Russia's police were tough, Madame Popova refused to confess initially. As the pressure mounted, she admitted, at last, to more than three hundred murders in thirty years. She was not sorry, and she refused to turn in anyone who had worked for her or reveal the names of her clients. She was found guilty and executed. Reports of her execution— like those of her murders—are sketchy, so little is known about how she died. But does it really matter? Like her victims, Madame Popova was quite dead.

PEARL HART

MAMA'S WILD CHILD

PEARL HART loved two things: the Wild West and her mother. Pearl began life as a good girl, attractive and full of wit. Born in Canada to a well-off family, she went to the finest schools. But alas, the good girl met a bad man—a heavy-drinking, not-so-nice gambler named Frederick Hart. She married him.

Once she smartened up, Pearl ran off to Colorado to get away from her abusive husband. But finding herself pregnant, she returned home to leave her new baby boy with her mother. Pearl wanted to work for a Wild West show, but that no-good husband kept finding her and promising to change. Another baby followed.

Three years later, Hart left her and the children and

enlisted in the army. So Pearl returned home, handed over her kids to her mother, and went out West again, this time to work in the Arizona mining camps as a cook.

In 1899 a letter arrived saying her mother was sick and needed money for her medical bills. One of the miners, Big Joe Boot, suggested they rob a stagecoach.

Pearl immediately loved the idea. It was so . . . Wild West! She chopped off her hair, put on men's clothes, and off they went. After they relieved the three passengers of four hundred dollars, Pearl felt bad so she returned a dollar to each, "for grub and lodging."

The bandits were soon captured and put in a Tucson jail. The newspapers had a heyday with the story. People felt sorry for Pearl because of her sick mother. She was given a lot of freedom in jail. So she escaped but was soon recaptured and sent to Yuma.

In interviews, Pearl, the only woman to ever rob a stagecoach, said she would not consent to be tried by laws made by men. She was pardoned in 1902 by the governor, and there were rumors that she had taken up with a bunch of pickpockets, or had become an actress, or was living happily ever after on a ranch with a cowboy named Calvin Bywater. But truth be told, she was never reliably heard from again.

TYPHOID MARY

A COOK WITHOUT A CONSCIENCE

MISTRESS MARY, quite contrary, how many folks did you kill? Thousands? That would make her a monster. Hundreds—still horrible. For years people believed this of her. However, the number of people Mary Mallon infected with deadly typhoid was merely in double digits, and only a handful actually died.

Mary Mallon was an Irish immigrant who came to America looking for a better life. She arrived in her mid teens and began earning a living, first as a maid and then as a cook for some of the best families in New York City. Her signature dish: peaches and cream.

But in 1906, life changed for Mary forever. The Long Island family she was cooking for came down with typhoid fever, a nasty bacterial infection that can kill if not treated quickly. First the daughter fell ill, then the mother and two maids, followed swiftly by the gardener and a second daughter. Altogether six of the eleven people in the house fell terribly ill. Fearing for her own safety—she didn't want to get sick too—Mary did what any healthy person in a house of sick people would do. She left. Quickly.

The family hired George Soper, a civil engineer who was experienced with typhoid outbreaks. Since typhoid is often spread through food, he focused right away on the family's cook. But she was gone. So he started researching her life.

What he found was strange indeed: typhoid seemed to follow Mary Mallon. In the seven places she had worked, twenty-two people had become ill where she worked. One young girl had died.

Was this a coincidence? Soper didn't think so.

The problem was that Mary Mallon had never been sick a day in her life. All her employers agreed that even in the midst of the typhoid outbreaks, Mary was singularly untouched by illness. Soper needed blood samples from Mary to find out if she was, indeed, a carrier of the disease.

Soper was able to follow her trail. A year later, in

March of 1907, he finally found her. Walking into her kitchen, he asked for blood samples. He told Mary calmly that he suspected she was making people sick. Not on purpose, but because of something in her blood.

Mary was frightened. Perhaps she didn't believe him. Maybe she thought he was trying to get her in trouble. Picking up a carving knife, she chased Soper out of her kitchen.

Later he brought backup, but she threatened both men, screaming and swearing at them.

Not looking for a third encounter with Mary's carving knife, Soper turned the case over to the New York City Health Department, which sent an ambulance, a doctor, and five strong police officers to get those samples.

This time Mary armed herself with a long kitchen fork. She managed to escape by climbing over a fence and into a neighbor's yard, where she was finally apprehended in a closet under an outside stairway.

Poor Mary. Though she had never been ill herself, tests proved she'd been serving up a side dish of typhoid to the families who ate her meals.

The health department said the problem was an infection of the gallbladder. They offered surgery to cure her—for free. But Mary refused. How did she know they weren't really planning to kill her? It all sounded to her like a made-up tale.

Since Mary refused treatment, all the health department could do was commit her to a small hospital on North Brother Island in New York City's East River for several years, hoping the bacteria would die out on its own. She was not at all happy about her imprisonment.

Finally, in 1909, Mary was let out on the condition that she never again work with food. But she was a cook. It gave her the status she craved. So she changed her name and returned to cooking.

Six years later during an outbreak of typhoid in Sloane Maternity Hospital in Manhattan, twenty-five people got sick, and two died. The outbreak was traced back to the cook, Mrs. Brown. But she wasn't Mrs. Brown: she was Mary Mallon. No one had checked her credentials.

So Mary was recaptured and sent back to the island, where she lived in quarantine for the last twenty-three years of her life. An autopsy revealed she was still carrying the disease, though no one was ever again served her peaches and cream with its very deadly secret ingredient—typhoid fever.

MATA HARI

THE SPY WHO LOVED EVERYONE

POOR M'GREET. This dark-eyed Dutch beauty had a rough life. When she was thirteen her family lost their money and she had to sell all her lovely things. Her mother died, and her father couldn't take care of her. She was too tall. She was too skinny. Just before she turned nineteen, she answered an ad in the paper and wound up with a dreadful, thirty-eight-year-old, abusive husband who drank too much and kept girl-friends on the side.

They had two children—a boy and a girl—but one horrible night the kids were poisoned and her son died. Still reeling from the mysterious loss of her son, M'greet finally divorced her husband. But after an ugly custody battle, the ex-husband took their daughter. Poor M'greet found herself without a home, family, or job.

In 1905 Margaretha Geertruida Zelle, once called M'greet by her family, changed her name to Mata Hari, made up an elaborate history for herself—she was the exotic daughter of a Javanese princess, who had studied sacred Indian dance since childhood—and became a dancer in Paris. Mata Hari quickly became the talk of the town. She danced beautifully, stripping down to almost nothing save her signature jeweled bra.

As Mata Hari, she caught the eyes of thousands of adoring men—and the hearts of a few as well. Her many boyfriends were rich and powerful men, including politicians and military officers from many countries. They took good care of her, and soon she was traveling all over Europe.

Poor M'greet was poor no more.

Here is where Mata Hari's story gets confusing. Times were changing, and World War I was brewing. Now living in Germany, Mata Hari was getting older. She had stopped dancing regularly.

There was talk. It was whispered that Mata Hari was a spy. The Germans claimed she was working for them. The French were sure she was squarely on their side. The British thought she was a spy for both Germany *and* France. No one doubted that Mata Hari could get information out of men. She was, after all, the most famous seductress of her time. But a spy? How scandalous! How delicious!

After leaving Germany just before the war began, the notorious Mata Hari, at age forty, fell in love with a young Russian officer named Vladimir Masloff. She wanted to stop seeing other men and be only with her true love. But Masloff had been wounded in battle, and they needed money. The only way Mata Hari could get money quickly, she thought, was to use her many contacts and become the spy she was already rumored to be. After all, spying could be very lucrative if done right. Why not give it a try?

Unfortunately Mata Hari was a much better dancer than she was a spy. She bumbled her way around the spy world, angering just about everyone. The secret German information she passed to the French was not so secret. Still, it made the Germans mad. The Germans reported that she was passing French information to them, something the French didn't find charming at all.

Suddenly everyone was furious with Mata Hari.

In 1917 Mata Hari was arrested as a German spy. The French, it seemed, wanted her to stop telling their secrets. After refusing a blindfold and blowing a kiss to her firing squad, Mata Hari—M'greet Zelle—was executed on October 15, 1917. She was only forty-one years old.

MA BARKER

MOTHER KNOWS WORST

MA BARKER loved her boys. When they were little, she loved them so much she wouldn't let anyone—even their own father—discipline them. When they were grown, she screamed, cried, and threw tantrums when anyone—even the police—tried to punish them.

Yes, Ma Barker loved her boys.

Arizona Clark, called Kate, was born into a religious family in the early 1870s. She married George Barker, and they had four sons: Herman, Lloyd, Arthur (called Doc), and her favorite, the youngest, Freddie. With no discipline, the Barker boys started acting up. When anyone dared to tell Ma Barker her boys were bad, she would hear nothing of it. The way she saw it, the world was out to get her perfect sons.

The boys' petty crimes soon turned into felonies. When they were arrested, Ma's tantrums just got bigger. She begged police officers and judges, government officials and jailers, to go easy on them. And sometimes her boys got out early because of it. The Barkers moved a couple of times to get away from persecutors and prosecutors. But as it usually does, trouble followed them.

The boys stole cars. They robbed banks, post offices, and stores. They were in jail and out. Finally they started killing people. All the while Ma Barker stood by them.

It went on this way until Ma's oldest boy, Herman, got into a gunfight with the police in 1927. He shot himself dead rather than be sent back to prison. Ma was devastated.

With her remaining sons in various prisons and her husband long gone, Ma Barker spent the next four years trying to spring the boys. Despite her efforts, Lloyd remained in the Leavenworth federal penitentiary. Doc was stuck on "The Rock" at Alcatraz. Only Freddie got out, making parole along with his best friend, Alvin Karpis. Ma had her favorite boy back. And she "adopted" Alvin. The crime spree began again, running from 1931 until 1935.

In St. Paul, Minnesota, Ma and the boys posed as

the Musical Andersons. In their violin cases they carried tommy guns. As the Barker-Karpis gang planned their next bank robbery, a neighbor recognized a picture of them in the magazine *True Detective Mysteries*. They barely escaped capture.

Though wanted by the law, Ma and her boys were rich from all their robberies. The new gang—including Ma—was living large. This meant they needed more money. But robbery had become too dangerous a business. Kidnapping, they thought, would be safer and more profitable. So they nabbed a wealthy man named William Hamm and ransomed him for $100,000. It was such a success that they planned a second kidnapping. Grabbing banker Edward Bremer, they demanded $200,000.

Bad plan.

Bremer's father was a friend of President Franklin Delano Roosevelt's, and Roosevelt put the country on high alert. The FBI, the police, postal workers, and ordinary citizens were soon looking for the kidnappers. After Bremer's ransom was paid, a fingerprint belonging to one of the boys was found. In an attempt to evade capture, Freddie and Alvin tried to change their faces and fingerprints with plastic surgery.

When that didn't work (and it hurt a *lot!*), they killed the surgeon.

The Barker-Karpis gang scattered. Freddie took Ma to Florida, where he became obsessed with hunting a three-legged alligator named Old Joe. Following a tip about the gator, the FBI traced Old Joe to Lake Weir. There they surrounded the outlaws' cabin. At a dawn shootout, Ma Barker and Freddie were outgunned and outmanned. More than two thousand rounds later, the lawmen ran out of ammunition. Only then did they realize the shooting from the cabin had stopped. Freddie and his doting Ma were upstairs dead. They were still clasping their guns.

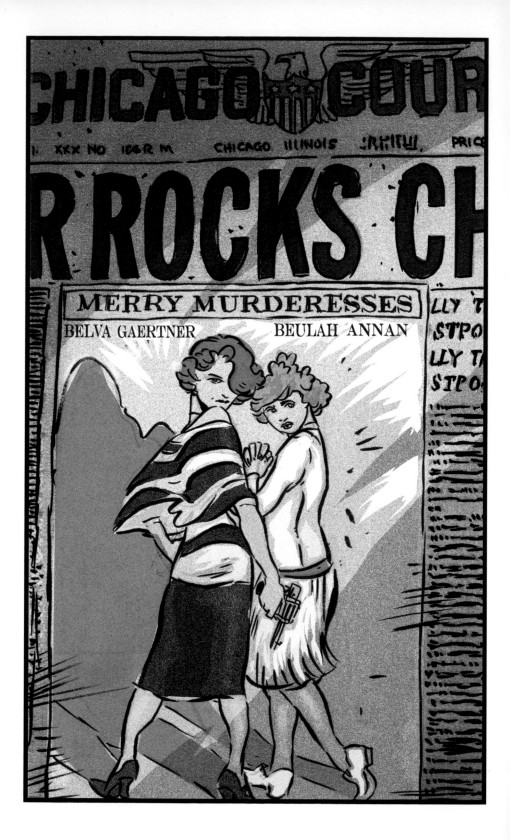

BEULAH ANNAN AND BELVA GAERTNER

CHICAGO'S MERRY MURDERESSES

BEULAH ANNAN

CIRCA 1901–1928

"I'm gonna be a celebrity,
that means somebody everyone knows . . ."

THIS IS THE SONG and desire of Roxie Hart, a character in the musical *Chicago*. Because she murders her lover and convinces her dim-witted husband to stick by her, Roxie does, indeed, become a celebrity.

In real life, Beulah Annan, the woman on whom the

character Roxie Hart is based, became a celebrity in 1924 when she killed her lover, Harry Kalstedt. The cheating couple ran around together for months before having a falling-out. When Kalstedt was found dead in her bedroom, Beulah claimed she had shot him in self-defense.

Probably closer to the truth was that Kalstedt was breaking up with her and she flew into a jealous rage. Or perhaps, as she claimed at her trial, they both reached for the gun during a struggle and when it went off, only she was left standing. The real truth really didn't matter.

Her trial was the big news of the day. Oh, the drama! Beulah claimed that she was pregnant with her husband's child. Either dim-witted or just plain gullible, he withdrew all the money from his bank account to hire William O'Brien, the best mob lawyer in town. O'Brien made sure Beulah had the best press and wore the prettiest clothes to influence the all-male jury. She flirted. She cried. She won them over. And when the prettiest girl on Murderess Row was acquitted and released, she divorced her husband and ran off to marry someone else.

The prosecutors were dismayed. They knew she was

guilty. But it was not to be their only disappointment in the spring of 1924. Another Chicago murderess was about to come to trial.

BELVA GAERTNER
CIRCA 1885-1965

"He had it coming," sings Velma Kelly in *Chicago's* "Cell Block Tango," about killing her husband. And perhaps he did. "It was a murder, but not a crime."

The character Velma Kelly is based on a real-life divorced cabaret singer named Belva Gaertner. It was almost spring in 1924, and Belva was having a rocky and volatile affair with a younger married man named Walter Law. Walter had told his friends that Belva was so jealous that he was sure she would eventually kill him. So when he showed up dead of a gunshot wound in Belva's car after a night of partying, the police didn't waste much time in tracking her down.

What they got was Belva and her blood-stained clothes. What they didn't get was a confession. She claimed not to remember anything except drinking and partying. Or was it the car and a loud noise? She kept changing her story. She liked Walter Law fine, she told the press, but "no woman can love a man enough to kill him. They aren't worth it, because there are always plenty more."

Belva's lawyer claimed that Law could have killed himself, but it probably wasn't his legal counsel that got Belva off. During the trial, she was all class. Everyone wanted to hear about her! The papers reported what she was wearing as much as what she said. In the end, though she faced the death penalty, the jury set her free. She lived until she was eighty.

THE REPORTER AND THE PLAY

Chicago Tribune reporter Maurine Watkins interviewed both Beulah and Belva in 1924 and made them famous. Though circumstance was their only relationship, the young reporter used booze and jazz to link the two women together, capturing the attention of her readers and keeping them riveted. But she didn't stop there. After Beulah and Belva were acquitted, Maurine, playing fast and loose with names and details, wrote a play about them called *Chicago*. When it opened in 1926, Belva attended the premiere. Later that play became a Broadway musical and an Oscar-winning movie.

BONNIE PARKER

CLYDE'S GIRL

IT MAY HAVE BEEN the Great Depression, but Bonnie Parker wasn't depressed. She was in love.

A petite, pretty Texan, Bonnie Parker first met Clyde Barrow in 1930, when she was just nineteen years old. Though she was young, she was already married to a bad boy by the name of Roy Thornton. But Roy was in prison for murder. Lonely Bonnie, who still wore Roy's ring and had a tattoo bearing his name, fell hard for Clyde.

And that's where the trouble began.

Clyde was already wanted by the law. But Bonnie didn't care. She liked bad boys. So when Clyde got himself locked up, Bonnie stole a gun and smuggled it into the prison for Clyde's jailbreak.

Clyde was quickly recaptured, but Bonnie promised to wait for him, even though his fourteen-year sentence seemed like forever. Clyde, too, couldn't stand to be away from his beloved for that long. Plus, he hated the hard work he was forced to do in prison. Clyde convinced a fellow inmate to cut off two of Clyde's toes, and though the injury did not get him out of all work duty, he was out of jail in two years because he wasn't strong enough to do the heavy jobs.

Once Clyde was free, Bonnie was again by his side. Soon Bonnie began acting as a lookout for Clyde and his ever-changing gang of hoodlums. She even did some time herself.

But that didn't stop her.

The killings started as an accident. A botched robbery and nervous outlaws with shaky fingers netted the gang one dead body. More followed. Now they were on the run. The law was after them, and the Barrow Gang stayed one step ahead by robbing, stealing, kidnapping, and even killing. They outgunned the police and always shot first, sometimes without so much as a warning.

And their legend grew. How it grew! Bonnie's presence in the gang captured the nation's attention.

Photographs they took of themselves on the road were found by the police and released to the press. Always conscious of her image, Bonnie asked one kidnapped police officer to tell everyone she did not smoke cigars, even though she had posed with one in her mouth. She may have been an outlaw, but she was not a smoker!

Beaten down by the Depression, the American public was riveted by tales of the gang. Bonnie and Clyde were the ultimate bad guys. But they were also the ultimate heroes, doing what many destitute Americans wished they could do—sticking it to the system that had failed them.

Life on the run wasn't easy. The gang tried to settle into an apartment, but that ended in a shootout with police that left two officers dead and two others seriously wounded. Later, when a getaway car crashed, Bonnie was pinned underneath while it exploded into flames. Too well known by then, she couldn't go to a hospital.

But not even Bonnie's injury slowed down the Barrow Gang. Their crime spree continued. They robbed and murdered their way through Texas, Oklahoma, Missouri, New Mexico, and Louisiana. In a gunfight with police, most of the rest of the gang was injured and Clyde's brother was killed. Bonnie and Clyde escaped to rebuild their gang, which included breaking old friends out of prison and killing a guard in the process.

But this was the beginning of the end. The reputation of Bonnie and Clyde had grown too large—they had to be stopped.

The big gun called in to do the stopping was a man named Frank Hamer. He swore he would find Bonnie and Clyde. He would shoot to kill. And like the gang, he would not give any warning.

Hamer tracked the outlaws and set a trap. When Bonnie and Clyde stopped to help a friend on the side of the road, Hamer and his hidden police posse opened fire on the outlaws, shooting round after round after round with their machine guns and stopping only when Bonnie and Clyde were both dead. Bonnie Parker was twenty-three years old.

VIRGINIA HILL

GANGSTER GIRLFRIEND

SOME GIRLS DREAM of being the girlfriend of a rich, powerful, famous man. Some girls dream of a career. Virginia Hill made a career out of being the girlfriend. Of the mob.

Virginia was born in the South and stuck around only long enough to decide she wanted to be famous. She was quite beautiful—a dancer with ambitions to become a movie star.

So she headed to Chicago.

In Chicago she met an accountant for the notorious gangster Al Capone. He was only her first in a string of mob men.

What Virginia was really good at, it turned out, was keeping her good fellas happy. Her womanly charms, accompanied by her willingness to carry money to Swiss bank accounts and her ability to keep a secret, made her the perfect girlfriend for more than a couple of bad boyfriends. They called her Flamingo.

And then she met Bugsy Siegel. Though she was not his only girlfriend, she was his favorite. And though he was not her first gangland boyfriend, he was *her* favorite.

Siegel named his hotel after her—the Flamingo.

After a while a rumor floated around gangland that Virginia and Bugsy had sneaked off and gotten married in Mexico.

Virginia continued carrying money to Europe for Bugsy, while he stole it from the mob and anywhere else he could find it. It was a dangerous venture, but with Virginia at his side, Bugsy did it with ease. And often.

They were quite a pair.

Even though she could keep a secret, it was well known that Virginia had mob ties. She had enough money in her handbag to buy her family a house with cash—more than $10,000, which is a lot of money to have in your purse.

But no one asked questions. Why would they, when the gifts were as big as a house? And Virginia bought herself houses in California, where she made a little extra money on the side by blackmailing rich celebrities.

She became a very rich woman.

Virginia's temper was legendary. Once she nearly broke the jaw of a woman she caught with her man. Later she slugged a reporter while screaming that she hoped the atom bomb would fall on the whole group that surrounded her.

But this temper did little to dampen Virginia's relationship with Bugsy. The pair fought and made up in a ferocious manner. In fact, their last fight, in 1947, resulted in Virginia storming off and boarding a plane to Paris.

While Virginia cooled her jets in France, Bugsy was murdered gangland-style on Virginia's living-room sofa. The fight actually saved her life.

Or maybe not.

People whispered that Virginia had known the hit was going down and had left town to save herself. After all, there were many gangsters who knew and loved

Virginia. Why wouldn't one of them have tipped her off?

When told of her beloved Bugsy's mafia execution, Virginia did what any smart girlfriend of the mob would do. She said she barely knew him. She lied.

"I'M NOT BAD.

I'M JUST DRAWN THAT WAY."

—Jessica Rabbit in

Who Framed Roger Rabbit

CONCLUSION

MODERN TIMES AND CHANGING
GENDER ROLES

IF SALOME dropped her veils today, would we call her bad? Or would we arrest her parents for a variety of crimes against a child? If Mata Hari made up a whole new self tomorrow and danced her way into a criminal lifestyle, would we execute her or send her to counseling for post-traumatic stress disorder? Would we encourage Lizzie Borden to move into her own apartment, Bloody Mary to establish an ecumenical council, and Typhoid Mary to take some nursing courses at a community college? Would we still consider these women bad? Or would we consider them victims of bad circumstances? As our world changes, so does our definition of *bad*. Especially when it comes to half the world's population—the half that happens to be female.

With women's relatively new rights—to speak out, to vote, to have power over their own bodies—comes a new set of responsibilities. Women are no longer required to do a man's bidding—no matter whether that bidding is legal or not. But no longer can a woman say that she was just following a man and count that as justification for bad acts.

We measure guilt and innocence today on a sliding scale. And never has it been easier for the general public to "weigh" the misdeeds of its favorite modern-day bad girls. The nightly news, tabloids, blogs, and the fast pace of the Internet all make sure of this. Today, as throughout history, the court of public opinion is capable of swaying or tempering the criminal courts.

Now that you have been introduced to some of history's bad girls, you will have to decide for yourself if they were really bad, not so bad, or somewhere in the middle. And perhaps you will see that even the baddest of bad girls may have had a good reason for what she did.

BIBLIOGRAPHY

DELILAH

Billinghurst, Jane. *Temptress.* Vancouver, BC: Greystone Books, 2004.

Frymer-Kensky, Tikva. *Reading the Women of the Bible.* New York: Schocken Books, 2002.

King James Bible, Judges 13–16

Knight, Kevin, ed. "Delilah." The Catholic Encyclopedia. http://www.newadvent.org/cathen/04605a.htm

Levi, Gerson B., Emil G. Hirsch, and Eduard König. "Delilah." Jewish Encyclopedia.com. http://jewishencyclopedia.com/articles/5062=delilah

JEZEBEL

Frymer-Kensky, Tikva. *Reading the Women of the Bible.* New York: Schocken Books, 2002.

Higgs, Liz Curtis. *Really Bad Girls of the Bible.* Colorado Springs, CO: Waterbrook Press, 2000.

Jastrow, Morris, Jr., J. Frederic McCurdy, and Duncan B. McDonald. "Ba-al and Ba-al Worship." JewishEncyclopedia.com. http://www.jewishencyclopedia.com/articles/2236-ba-al-and-ba-al-worship

CLEOPATRA

Grant, Michael. *Cleopatra.* New York: Simon & Schuster, 1972.

Jones, Constance. *1001 Things Everyone Should Know About Women's History.* New York: Doubleday, 1998.

Stanley, Diane. *Cleopatra.* New York: Morrow Junior Books, 1994.

Suetonius Tranquillus, Caius. The Lives of the Twelve Caesars. http://penelope.uchicago.edu/Thayer/E/Roman/Texts/Suetonius/12Caesars/Julius*.html

SALOME

Frymer-Kensky, Tikva. *Reading the Women of the Bible.* New York: Schocken Books, 2002.

Higgs, Liz Curtis. *Really Bad Girls of the Bible.* Colorado Springs, CO: Waterbrook Press, 2000.

ANNE BOLEYN

Farquhar, Michael. *A Treasury of Royal Scandals.* New York: Penguin Books, 2001.

Fraser, Antonia. *The Wives of Henry VIII.* New York: Knopf, 1992.

Mattingly, Garrett. *Catherine of Aragon.* New York: Book-of-the-Month-Club, 1941.

BLOODY MARY

"Bloody Mary." Wikipedia. http://en.wikipedia.org/wiki/Mary_I_of_England

Eakins, Lara E. "Mary I: Queen of England." Tudorhistory.org. http://tudorhistory.org/mary/queen.html

Fraser, Antonia. *The Wives of Henry VIII.* New York: Knopf, 1992.

Kamen, Henry. *Philip of Spain.* New Haven: Yale University Press, 1997.

Lindbuchler, Ryan. "Queen 'Bloody' Mary I Tudor of England." Prof.
Pavlac's Women's History Resource Site.
http://departments.kings.edu/womens_history/marytudor.html.

ELISABETH BÁTHORY

Howard, Amanda, and Martin Smith. *River of Blood: Serial Killers & Their
Victims.* Boca Raton, FL: Universal Publishers, 2004.

Newton, Michael. *Bad Girls Do It! An Encyclopedia of Female Murderers.*
Port Townsend, WA: Loompanics Unlimited, 1993.

Uglow, Jennifer S., comp. and ed. *The Northeastern Dictionary of Women's
Biography.* Boston: Northeastern University Press, 1982.

MOLL CUTPURSE

Harper, Charles G. *Half-hours with the Highwaymen.* Vol 1. London:
Chapman & Hall, Limited, 1908.

"Mary Frith otherwise Moll Cutpurse." *The Complete Newgate Calendar.*
Vol. 1. Tarlton Law Library.

Moore, Lucy. *The Thieves' Opera.* New York: Harcourt Brace, 1998.

Spraggs, Gillian, researcher, private letter about Moll to Jane Yolen, 1997.

Whibley, Charles. *A Book of Scoundrels.* New York: E. P. Dutton & Co., 1912.

TITUBA

Barillari, Alyssa. "Tituba." Salem Witch Trials: Documentary Archive and
Transcription Project.
http://www.iath.virginia.edu/salem/people/tituba.html

Breslaw, Elaine G. *Tituba: Reluctant Witch of Salem.* New York and
London: New York University Press, 1996.

Discovery Education. *"Tituba." Salem Witch Trials: The World Behind
the Hysteria.*
http://school.discovery.com/schooladventures/salemwitchtrals/people/
tituba.html

Hill, Frances. *A Delusion of Satan.* New York: De Capo Press, Inc., 1995.

"Salem Witchcraft Trials 1692: Tituba." Famous Trials.
   http://www.law.umkc.edu/faculty/projects/ftrials/salem/ASA_TIT.HTM

Wilson, Lori Lee. *How History Is Invented: The Salem Witch Trials.*
   Minneapolis, MN: Lerner Publications Company, 1997.

Yolen, Jane, and Heidi Elisabet Yolen Stemple. *The Salem Witch Trials: An
   Unsolved Mystery from History.* New York: Simon & Schuster, 2004.

ANNE BONNEY AND MARY READ

Carse, Robert. *The Age of Piracy.* New York: Rinehart & Winston, 1957.

Cordingly, David. *Under the Black Flag: The Romance and the Reality of
   Life Among the Pirates.* New York: Random House, 1995.

Druett, Joan. *She Captains: Heroines and Hellions of the Sea.* New York:
   Simon & Schuster, 2000.

Gosse, Philip, *The History of Piracy.* London: Longmans, Green & Company, 1932.

Johnson, Cathy. *Pyrates in Petticoats: A Fanciful & Factual History of the
   Legends, Tales, and Exploits of the Most Notorious Female Pirates.*
   Excelsior Springs, MO: Graphics/Fine Arts Press, 2000.

Johnson, Captain Charles. *A General History of the Robberies and Murders of the Most Notorious Pirates.* London: Routledge & Kegan Paul,
   Ltd., 1926, 1955.

Klausmann, Ulrike, Marion Meinzerin, and Gabriel Kuhn. *Women Pirates and
   the Politics of the Jolly Roger.* Montreal, QC: Black Rose Books, 1997.

Rediker, Marcus. *Between the Devil and the Deep Blue Sea: Merchant
   Seamen, Pirates, and the Anglo-American Maritime World 1700–
   1750.* Cambridge, UK: Cambridge University Press, 1987.

Yolen, Jane. *Pirates in Petticoats.* New York: David McKay Company, Inc., 1963.

Yolen, Jane. *Sea Queens.* Watertown, MA: Charlesbridge, 2008.

PEGGY SHIPPEN ARNOLD

Boatner, Mark M., III. *Encyclopedia of the American Revolution.* Mechanicsburg, PA: Stackpole Books, 1994.

"Peggy Shippen." Wikipedia.
http://en.wikipedia.org/wiki/Peggy_Shippen

"A Tragic Life." Society of Stukely Westcott Descendants of America.
http://old.sswda.org/Archives/People/Bios/Arnold_Benedict.htm

CATHERINE THE GREAT

"Catherine II of Russia." Wikipedia.
http://en.wikipedia.org/wiki/Catherine_II_of_Russia

"Catherine and Peter: The Odd Couple." History House.
www.historyhouse.com/in_history/catherine_one

"Catherine the Great." About.com: Women's History.
http://womenshistory.about.com/od/catherinegreat/p/catherinegreat.htm

Farquhar, Michael, *A Treasury of Royal Scandals.* Penguin Books, 2001.

"The Princess Who Became . . . Catherine the Great." Ursula's History Web.
http://nevermore.tripod.com/CGREAT.HTM

ROSE O'NEAL GREENHOW

Farquhar, Michael. "'Rebel Rose,' A Spy of Grande Dame Proportions." *Washington Post,* September 18, 2000, A1.

"Rose O'Neal Greenhow." About.com: Women's History.
http://womenshistory.about.com/od/womenspiescivilwar/a/Rose-O-Neal-Greenhow.htm

"Rose O'Neal Greenhow, 1817–1864: Confederate Spy." AmericanCivilWar.com. http://americancivilwar.com/women/rg.html

BELLE STARR

Jones, Constance. *101 Things Everyone Should Know About Women's History.* New York: Broadway Books, 1998.

Lakewood Public Library. "Belle Starr." *Women in History: Living Vignettes of Notable Women from U.S. History.* http://www.lkwdpl.org/wihohio/star-bel.htm

CALAMITY JANE

"Calamity Jane." Wikipedia. http://en.wikipedia.org/wiki/Calamity_Jane

Frost, Edith. "Calamity Jane." Cowgirl's Dream. http://www.cowgirls.com/dream/cowgals/calamity.htm

Jones, Constance. *1001 Things Everyone Should Know About Women's History.* New York: Broadway Books, 2000.

Lewis, Jone Johnson. "Calamity Jane." About.com: Women's History. http://womenshistory.about.com/od/westernamerica/p/calamity_jane.htm

McLaird, James D. *Calamity Jane: The Woman and the Legend.* Norman, OK: The University of Oklahoma Press, 2005.

LIZZIE BORDEN

Aiuto, Russell. "Lizzie Borden Took an Axe." TruTV Crime Library. http://www.trutv.com/library/crime/notorious_murders/famous/borden/index_1.html

Axelrod-Contrada, Joan. *The Lizzie Borden "Axe Murder" Trial: A Headline Court Case.* Berkeley Heights, NJ: Enslow Publishers, Inc., 2000.

Linder, Douglas. "The Trial of Lizzie Borden, 1893." Famous Trials. http://law2.umkc.edu/faculty/projects/ftrials/LizzieBorden/bordenhome.html

Sullivan, Robert. *Goodbye Lizzie Borden.* London: Penguin Books, 1974.

MADAME ALEXE POPOVA

Geringer, Joseph. "Violence in Dulcet Tones." TruTV Crime Library.

http://www.trutv.com/library/crime/criminal_mind/psychology/widows/2.html

Howard, Amanda, and Martin Smith. *River of Blood: Serial Killers & Their Victims*. Boca Raton, FL: Universal Publishers, 2004.

Kelleher, Michael D., and C. L. Kelleher. *Murder Most Rare: The Female Serial Killer*. Westport, CT: Dell Publishing, 1998.

"Popova, Alexe." Serial Killer Crime Index.

http://www.crimezzz.net/serialkillers/P/POPOVA_alexe.php

PEARL HART

Jones, Constance. *1001 Things Everyone Should Know About Women's History*. New York: Broadway Books, 2000.

Machula, Paul R. "Pearl Hart." East Central Arizona History.

http://www.zybtarizona.com/pearl.htm

Woody, Clara T., and Milton L. Schwartz. *Globe, Arizona*. Tucson: Arizona Historical Society, 1977.

TYPHOID MARY

Jones, Constance. *1001 Things Everyone Should Know About Women's History*. New York: Broadway Books, 2000.

Kohn, George Childs. *The New Encyclopedia of American Scandal*. New York: Facts on File, 2001.

Leavitt, Judith Walzer. "Typhoid Mary: Villain or Victim?" *The Most Dangerous Woman in America*. NOVA.

http://www.pbs.org/wgbh/nova/body/typhoid-mary-villain-or-victim.html

NOVA. "In Her Own Words." The Most Dangerous Woman in America.

http://www.pbs.org/wgbh/nova/typhoid/letter.html

Rosenberg, Jennifer. "Typhoid Mary." About.com: 20th Century History.

http://history1900s.about.com/od/1900s/a/typhoidmary.htm

"Typhoid Fever." Wikipedia.

    http://en.wikipedia.org/wiki/Typhoid

MATA HARI

Duffy, Michael. "Who's Who: Mata Hari." FirstWorldWar.com.

    http://www.firstworldwar.com/bio/matahari.htm

"The Execution of Mata Hari, 1917." Eyewitness to History.

    http://www.eyewitnesstohistory.com/pfmatahari.htm

Jeffries, Stuart. "Did They Get Mata Hari Wrong?" *The Guardian,*
    October 16, 2001.

    http://www.guardian.co.uk/world/2001/oct/humanities.highereducation

"Mata Hari." FemBio.

    http://www.fembio.org/english/biography.php/woman/biography/mata-hari

"Mata Hari." Propaganda Postcards of the Great War.

    http://www.ww1-propaganda-cards.com/mata_hari.html

"Mata Hari." Wikipedia.

    http://en.wikipedia.org/wiki/Mata_Hari

Noe, Denise. "The Story of Mata Hari." TruTV Crime Library.

    http://www.trutv.com/library/crime/terrorists_spies/spies/hari/1.html

Platt, Richard. *Spy.* New York: Dorling Kindersley Publishing, Inc., 2000.

Ramirez, Ronnette. "A Glimpse of the Belly Dancer, Mata Hari." BellaOnline.

    http://www.bellaonline.com/articles/art45815.asp

"Was Mata Hari Framed?" *New York Times,* October 16, 2001.

    http://www.nytimes.com/2001/10/16/world/world-briefing-europe-
    france-was-mata-hari-framed.html

MA BARKER

Bevan, Richard. "Famous Criminals: Ma Barker:" Crime & Investigation
    Network.

    http://www.crimeandinvestigation.co.uk/crime-files/ma-barker/
    biography.html

Gazis-Sax, Joel. "'Doc' on the Rock: Ripples from the Fall of Arthur Barker." Tales from Colma.

http://www.notfrisco.com/colmatales/barker/index.html#mabarker

"Ma and Her Boys: One Family's Life of Crime."

http://www.notfrisco.com/colmatales/barker/barkertl.html

"Ma Barker." Wikipedia.

http://en.wikipedia.org/wiki/Ma_Barker

"Ma Barker: Crime Family Values." *A&E Biography.* A&E Television Networks, 1998.

Smith, Patterson. "Thomas McDade and *The Annals of Murder.*" AB Bookman's Weekly, April 22, 1996.

http://www.patterson-smith.com/mcdadeArt.htm

BEULAH ANNAN AND BELVA GAERTNER

"Belva Gaertner." Wikipedia.

http://en.wikipedia.org/wiki/Belva_Gaertner

"Beulah Annan." Wikipedia.

http://en.wikipedia.org/wiki/Beulah_Annan

Gupton, Nancy. "*Chicago:* The True Murders That Inspired the Movie." National Geographic News.

http://news.nationalgeographic.com/news/2003/03/0321_030321_oscars_chicago.html

BONNIE PARKER

Barrow, Blanche Caldwell. *My Life with Bonnie & Clyde.* Norman, OK: University of Oklahoma Press, 2004.

"Famous Cases: Bonnie and Clyde." Federal Bureau of Investigation.

http://www.fbi.gov/about-us/history/famous-cases/bonnie-and-clyde/bonnie-and-clyde

Geringer, Joseph. "Bonnie & Clyde: Romeo and Juliet in a Getaway Car." TruTV Crime Library.

http://www.trutv.com/library/crime/gangsters_outlaws/outlaws/bonnie/1.html

Milner, E. R. *The Lives and Times of Bonnie & Clyde.* Carbondale, IL: Southern Illinois University Press, 1996.

"Parker, Bonnie." The Handbook of Texas Online.
http://www.tshaonline.org/handbook/online/articles/fpa17.html

Rosa, Paul. "The Story of Bonnie and Clyde." HistoryBuff.com.
http://www.historybuff.com/library/refbonnie.html

Steele, Phillip W., with Marie Barrow Scoma. *The Family Story of Bonnie and Clyde.* Gretna, LA: Pelican Publishing Company, 2000.

VIRGINIA HILL

Gribben, Mark. "Virginia Hill: Girlfriend to the Mob." TruTV Crime Library.
http://www.trutv.com/library/crime/gangsters_outlaws/mob_bosses/women/3.html

Sifakis, Carl. *The Encyclopedia of American Crime.* New York: Facts on File, Inc., 2001.

"Virginia Hill." Wikipedia. http://en.wikipedia.org/wiki/Virginia_Hill

Publisher's Note

While the websites listed in this work were current upon publication, please keep in mind that some web addresses may relocate or expire over time.

INDEX

A

Ahab, 11–13
American War for Independence,
  69–70
André, John, 70–71
Annan, Beulah, 127–128,
  130–131
Antipas, Herod, 25–29
Antony, Mark, 20–21
Arnold, Benedict, 69–73
Arnold, Peggy Shippen, 69–73

B

Barker brothers, 121–123, 125
Barker, Ma, 121–125
Barrow, Clyde, 133–137
Báthory, Elisabeth, 3, 43–45
Beauregard, P. G. T., 81–82
Black Dogs, 48–49
blackmail, 141
Bloody Mary, 2, 33, 37–41, 145
Boleyn, Anne, 31–35, 37–39, 41

Boleyn, Thomas, 31
Bonney, Anne, 59–61, 63–67
Bonney, James, 60
Boot, Big Joe, 106
Borden, Abby, 95–96, 99
Borden, Andrew, 95–99
Borden, Emma, 95–96, 98
Borden, Lizzie, 2, 3, 95–99, 143,
  145
Bremer, Edward, 123
Bywater, Calvin, 106

C

Caesar, Julius, 18–20
Calamity Jane, 91–93
Cannary, Martha Jane, *see*
  Calamity Jane
Capone, Al, 139
Catherine of Aragon, 31, 37–38
Catherine the Great, 75–79
Catholic Church, 31, 33, 38–40
Charles I, 49

Charles II, 50

Chicago, 127, 129–131

Church of England, 33

Civil War, 81–83, 85, 89

Clark, Arizona, *see* Barker, Ma

Cleopatra, 17–23

Clinton, Hillary, 51

Cromwell, Oliver, 49

Cutpurse, Moll, 3, 47–51

D

Delilah, 5–9

divorce, 21, 33, 34, 37, 115, 128, 129

E

Edward VI, 39

Egypt, 17–23

Elijah, 13

Elizabeth I, 33, 38–41

England, 31–35, 37–41, 47–50, 69–73, 117

F

Figchen, *see* Catherine the Great

France, 116–118, 141

Frith, Mary, *see* Cutpurse, Moll

G

Gaertner, Belva, 129–131

Germany, 116–118

Great Depression, 121, 125, 133, 135

Greenhow, Rose O'Neal, 81–83

Grey, Jane, 39–40

H

Hamer, Frank, 136

Hamm, William, 123

Hari, Mata, 3, 115–119, 143, 145

Hart, Frederick, 105

Hart, Pearl, 2, 105–107

Henry VIII, 31–34, 37–39

Herodias, 25–29

Hill, Virginia, 139–143

I

Ivan VI, 77

J

Jezebel, 11–15

John the Baptist, 2, 26–28

July, Jim, 87

K

Kalstedt, Harry, 128

Karpis, Alvin, 123–125

kidnapping, 123, 134–135

L

Law, Walter, 129–130

Lepidus, Marcus, 20

M

Mallon, Mary, *see* Typhoid Mary

Mary I, *see* Bloody Mary

Masloff, Vladimir, 117

mob, 128, 139–143

Morse, John, 96

murder and killing, 2, 9, 28–29, 40, 43–45, 95–99, 101–103, 122, 124, 127–131, 134–136, 141

N

Naboth, 12

O

O'Brien, William, 128

Octavian, 20, 21

P

Parker, Bonnie, 133–137, 143

Parker, Isaac, 86

Parris, Betty, 53–54

Parris, Samuel, 53–56

Percy, Lord, 32

Peter III, 75–77, 79

Philip II, 40

piracy, 59–67

poison, 19, 21–22, 23, 96–97, 99, 101–102, 115

Popova, Madame Alexe, 101–103

Ptolemy XIII, 17–19

Ptolemy XIV, 19

Puritans, 49, 53–57

Q

Quantrill's Raiders, 85

R

Rackham, Calico Jack, 59–61, 63–65

Read, Mary, 59, 61–67

Reed, Jim, 86

religion, 11–15, 31, 33, 38–40, 53, 76

robbery and theft, 2, 48–50, 86–87, 106–107, 121–125, 134–135

Rogers, Woods, 64

Rome, 18–21, 25–26

Roosevelt, Franklin Delano, 123

Russia, 75–79, 101–102, 117

S

Salome, 2, 3, 25–29, 145

Samson, 5–9

Seymour, Jane, 34, 39

Shirley, Myra Maybelle, *see* Starr, Belle

Sibley, Mary, 55

Siegel, Bugsy, 140–143

Soper, George, 110–111

Spenlow, James, 64

spying, 70–73, 81–83, 85, 116–119, 143

Starr, Belle, 85–89

Starr, Sam, 86–87

T

Tarakanova, Princess, 77

Thornton, Roy, 133

Tituba, 53–57

Typhoid Mary, 109–113, 145

W

Washington, George, 70–72

Watkins, Maurine, 130

Watson, Edgar, 87

West Point, 70–71

Wild West, 92, 105–106

Williams, Abigail, 53–54

witchcraft, 31, 35, 43–45, 53–57

women's rights, 146

World War I, 116

Z

Zelle, Margaretha Geertruida, *see*
  Hari, Mata

JANE YOLEN
1939–?

Jane Yolen was born bad, the daughter of a couple of liars (er, writers). Most of her early lies were written in poor rhyme, but as she got older she also committed prose. Mother of three, grandmother of six, she forces her books on her nearest and dearest in the hope that they'll follow in her size-9 footsteps. She lives in western Massachusetts and Scotland.

www.janeyolen.com

HEIDI E. Y. STEMPLE
1966-?

Heidi Stemple knew that she wanted to be bad as early as high school. She studied criminal justice and then worked with crime victims and perpetrators. She tried to escape the lure of the family business, but in the end she succumbed, committing literary crimes with her mother, Ma Yolen. Heidi lives in an undisclosed location with two felonious daughters and two criminally insane cats.

www.heidieystemple.com

REBECCA GUAY
1970–?

Rebecca Guay has been committing crimes of fashion since she was a toddler. Her current misdeeds include random-but-sizeable social blunders and being criminally hard on her own work. Her life of crime and art continues in western Massachusetts to this day.

www.rebeccaguay.com